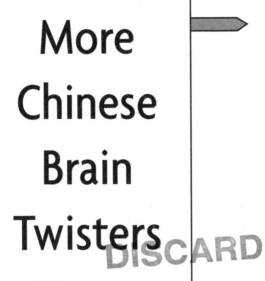

More Chinese Brain Twisters

57 Fast, Fun Puzzles That Help Children Develop Quick Minds

Baifang

John Wiley & Sons, Inc.

New York Chichester Weinheim Brisbane Singapore Toronto

This book is printed on acid-free paper. ∞

Published by John Wiley & Sons, Inc.
Published simultaneously in Canada

This publication is designed to provide accurate and authoritative information
in regard to the subject matter covered. It is sold with the understanding
that the publisher is not engaged in rendering legal, accounting, or other
professional services. If legal advice or other expert assistance is required,
the services of a competent professional person should be sought.

Library of Congress Cataloging-in-Publication Data:

Baifang
    More Chinese brain twisters: 57 fast, fun puzzles that help children
    develop quick minds / Baifang.
        p.   cm.
    ISBN 0-471-24613-1 (paper)
     1. Puzzles.   2. Amusement—China.   I. Title.
    GV1493.B2123   1999
    793.73—dc21   99-12224

Printed in the United States of America
10 9 8 7 6 5 4 3 2 1

More Chinese Brain Twisters

Contents

Introduction

There is wisdom in the old Chinese saying "Things learned during childhood remain with one forever." When I was growing up in the north of China during the 1950s and 1960s, my family and friends taught me how to do many of the puzzles included in this book. My parents later recalled others from their childhood in the 1930s and 1940s.

Such puzzles are part of China's folk culture. They have endured for centuries, even through the Communist era of Mao Zedong, when so many other traditional ways of life were lost. They speak of the commitment of Chinese parents to expand their children's intellectual capacities during even their earliest years.

I was very pleased that the first volume of this collection has been so well received and that the publisher was eager for another. I was happy to oblige. I hope you and your children enjoy these puzzles as much as I have.

Baifang

Instructions

The book is divided into two parts: Sticks and Shapes, and Lines, Shapes, and Numbers. Each contains puzzles that help develop agile, creative minds. These mental calisthenics will also help prepare your child for a lifetime of clear, logical thinking. Playing with real sticks allows your child to manipulate the concepts and leads to even greater learning.

Who can solve these puzzles?

Anyone above the age of eight can enjoy the puzzles. When I was a child, my family introduced me to the easiest ones first. As I learned how to solve them, I tried to remember the solutions so that I could solve them faster the next time I saw them.

Although your child may work his or her way through the book alone, it is much more fun to share the experience. You can do these puzzles together at any place, at almost any time—at home, on vacation, on a plane or train, or even while camping. One person can work on them alone, of course, or a group can turn them into a game by competing against each other or against the clock.

What do you need to solve the puzzles?

You'll need a pen or pencil, some paper, and a flat surface. You'll also need about fifty short sticks. Toothpicks or matchsticks are just the right length. You can also use straws cut into equal lengths, about two inches long.

To solve the puzzles, form the patterns with your sticks or draw them on a piece of paper.

Rules for the puzzles:

To **move** sticks means to shift the position of a stick without reducing the original number.

To **remove** a given number of sticks means to take away, thus reducing the number of sticks in the pattern.

To **add** means to increase a given number of sticks.

Let's try one stick puzzle together:

These **three** diamonds can be changed to **four** equilateral (equal-sided) triangles by moving **two** sticks. Which **two** should be moved?

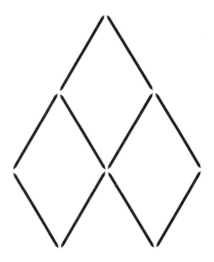

Turn the page to find the solution.

Start

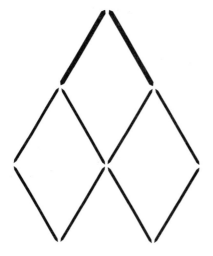

Here the thick lines show the sticks to be moved.

Finish

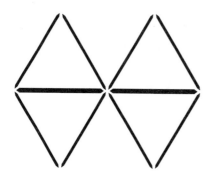

And here the thick lines show the new position of the moved sticks.

Now let's begin!

Sticks and Shapes

By moving **two** sticks, the pattern below can be changed into a dinner fork. Which **two** should be moved?

Start

Finish

Can you form **two** A's using only **four** sticks?

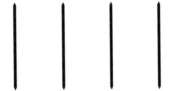

Start

Finish

Can you form **six** triangles and **one** diamond using only these **six** sticks?

Start

Finish

You can make the reflection of the pattern below by moving only **six** sticks. Which **six** need to be moved?

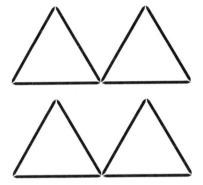

Start

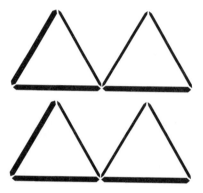

Finish

Please change the pattern on the top to the one on the bottom by moving only **three** sticks. Which **three** ought to be moved?

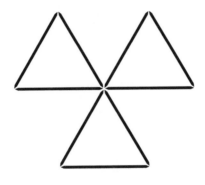

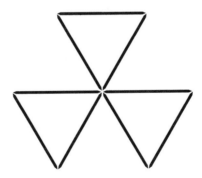

Start

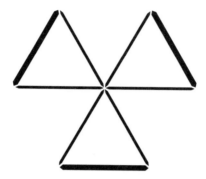

Finish

How can you form **one** square and **two** diamonds by using **nine** sticks?

Start

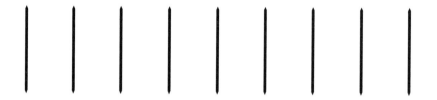

Finish

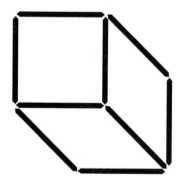

How can you use these **six** sticks to form **eight** triangles?

Start

Finish

How can you form **four** triangles by using only **six** sticks?

Start

Finish

By rearranging **ten** sticks, you can form **five** equal-size triangles and **two** pentagons. How do you do this?

Start

Finish

How can you use **twelve** sticks to form **two** squares and **two** diamonds?

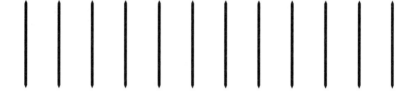

Start

Finish

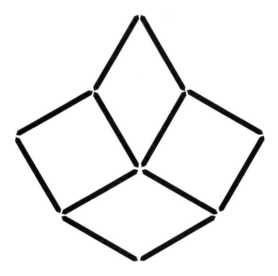

How can you turn the chair away from you by moving only **two** sticks?

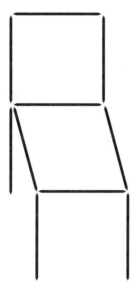

Start

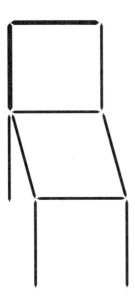

Finish

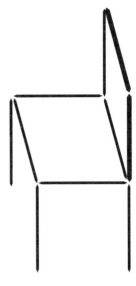

You can turn the chair over onto its back by moving only **three** sticks. Which **three** should be moved?

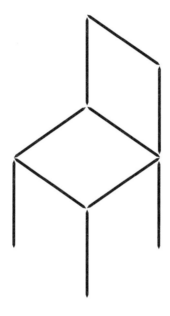

Start

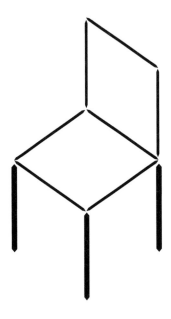

Finish

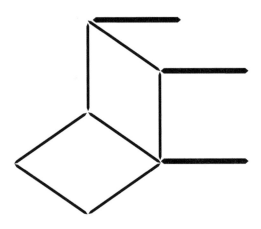

This dog was run over by a truck. By moving only **two** sticks, you can illustrate this unfortunate fact. Which **two** sticks should be moved?

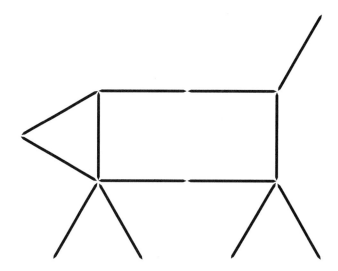

Start

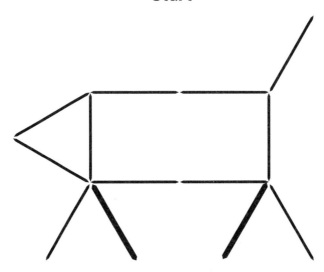

Finish

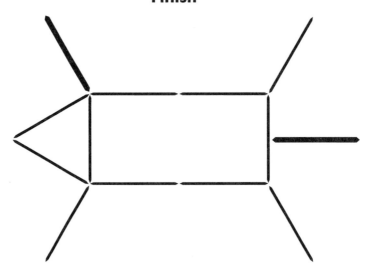

This big square is formed by **twelve** sticks. By adding **seven** more sticks, you can separate the square into **three** equal parts. Four of the **seven** are already in position. Where should the **three** remaining sticks go?

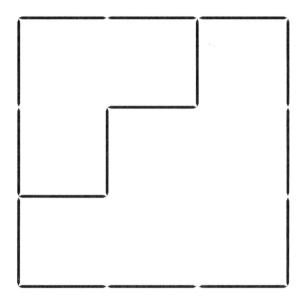

Start

Finish

This big shovel can be turned into **two** small shovels by moving **four** sticks. Which **four** need to be moved?

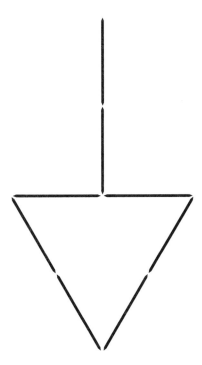

Start

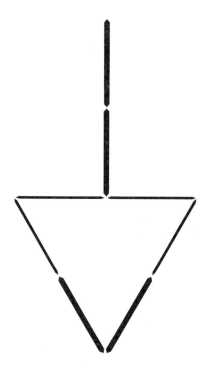

Finish

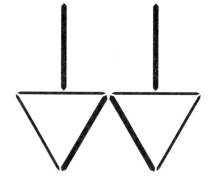

How can you change these **five** equal-size squares into **four** equal-size squares by moving only **four** sticks?

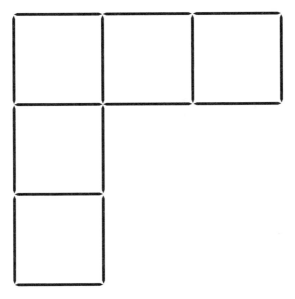

Start

Finish

You can change these **five** equal-size squares into **three** squares by moving only **four** sticks. Which **four** should be moved?

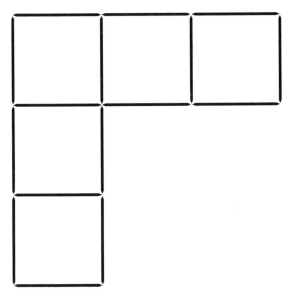

Start

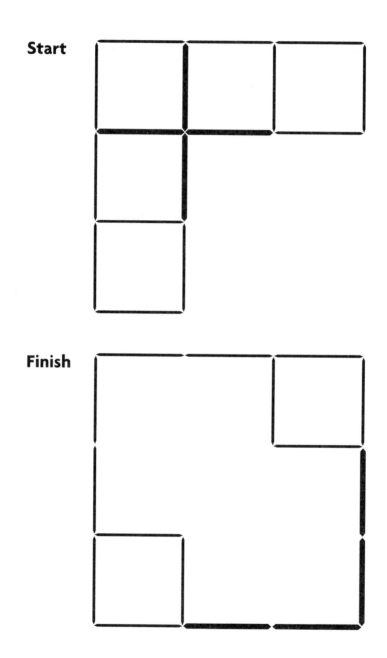

Finish

Forty sticks can be used to form a pattern made up of **sixteen** equal-size squares. By removing **eight** sticks, this pattern will have only **two** squares left. Which **eight** sticks should be removed?

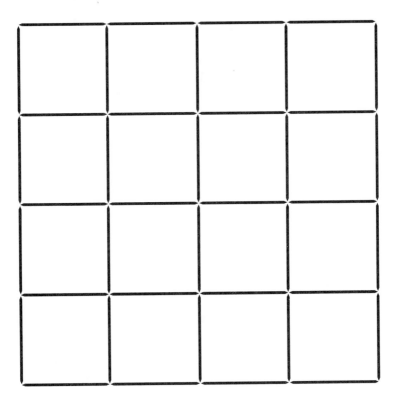

Start

Finish

How can you turn the pattern below upside down by moving only **four** sticks?

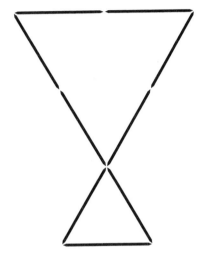

Start

Finish

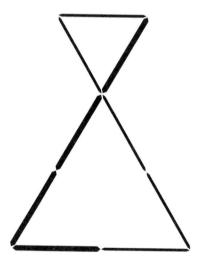

Here are **two** equal-size diamonds standing side by side. By moving **four** sticks, **one** diamond will disappear and **one** will grow. Which **four** sticks should be moved?

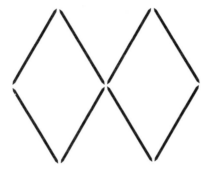

Start

Finish

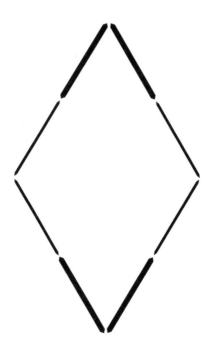

A pattern with **two** diamonds can be formed by using **seven** sticks. A pattern with **five** diamonds can be formed by using **twelve** sticks. How can you form a pattern with **three** diamonds by using **nine** sticks?

two diamonds

five diamonds

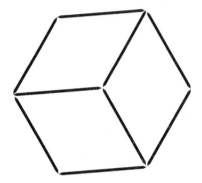

three diamonds (nine sticks)

The pattern below is formed by using **nine** sticks. By removing **two** sticks only **two** equilateral triangles will remain. Which **two** sticks should be removed?

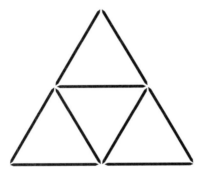

Start

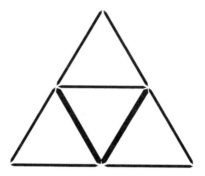

Finish

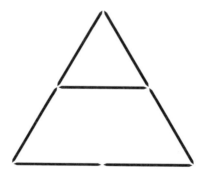

How can you make this kite fly in the opposite direction by moving only **four** sticks?

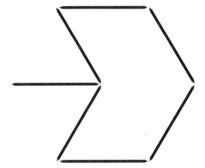

Start

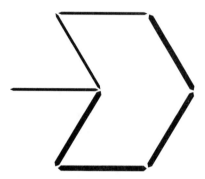

Finish

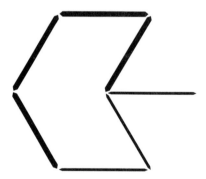

The pattern below is composed of **three** equilateral triangles and **two** squares. How can you rearrange these sticks to form exactly the same number of equilateral triangles and squares in a different pattern?

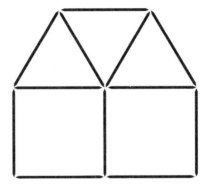

Start

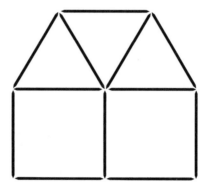

Finish

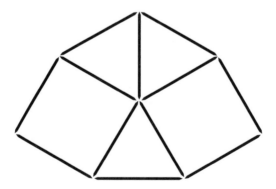

By moving only **three** sticks, the pattern below will turn upside down. Which **three** sticks should be moved?

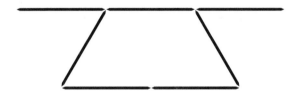

Start

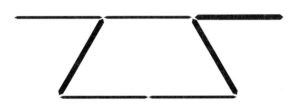

Finish

How can you transform this hexagon into **two** parallelograms by moving **two** sticks and adding **one** more stick?

Start

Finish

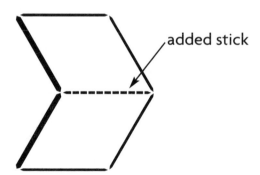

added stick

These **five** patterns are formed using same number of sticks. Which pattern has the largest area?

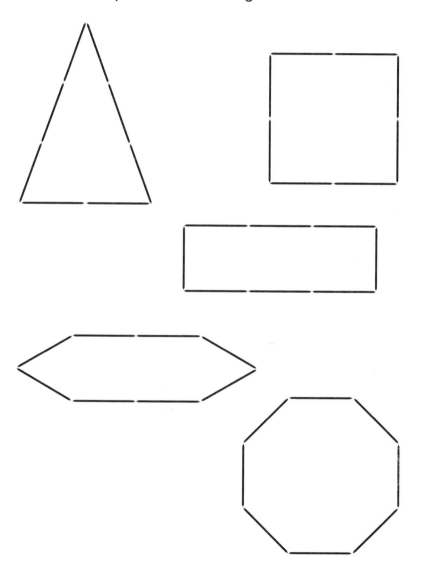

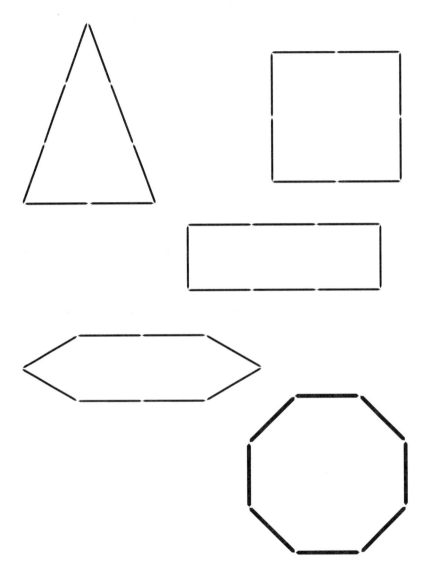

The pattern with a circumference closest to a circle has the largest area. Here the octagon is closest to a circle, so it has the largest area.

There are two ways of adding **six** more sticks to the pattern below so that it will emerge as a new pattern with **five** similarly shaped components. Where should the **six** sticks be placed?

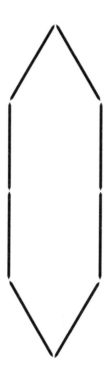

SOLUTION A
Start

SOLUTION B
Start

Finish

Finish

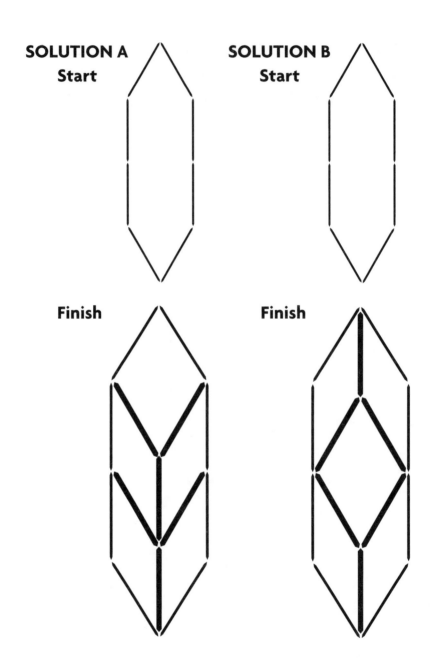

The pattern below has **six** diamonds in it. How can you remove **six** sticks and then resposition **six** other sticks so that the pattern still has **six** diamonds?

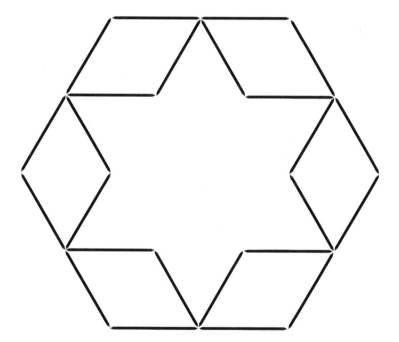

Start

Finish

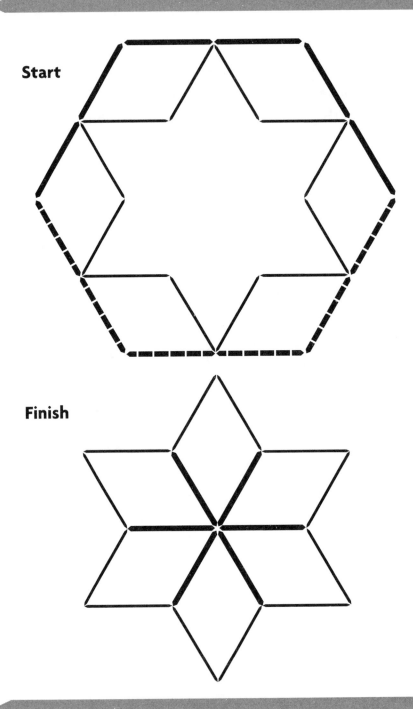

The pattern below contains **four** equal-size squares.

A. How do you remove **two** sticks so that it will turn into only **two** squares?

B. How do you move **three** sticks so it will turn into **three** squares?

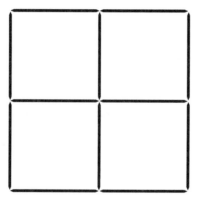

SOLUTION A
Start

SOLUTION B
Start

Finish

Finish

This spiral pattern is made up of **twenty-four** sticks. How do you move **three** sticks to turn the spiral into **three** squares?

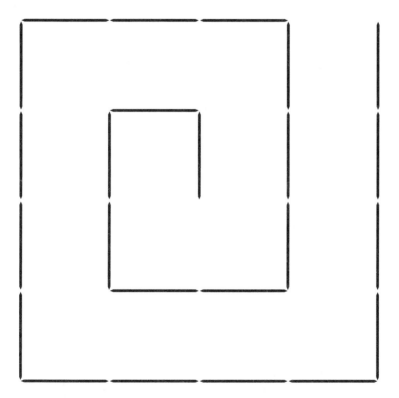

Start

Finish

The pattern below contains **seven** equal-size squares. If you move **three** sticks it turns into only **five** equal-size squares. Which **three** sticks should be moved?

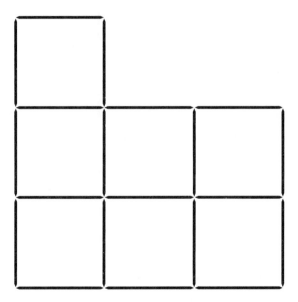

Start

Finish

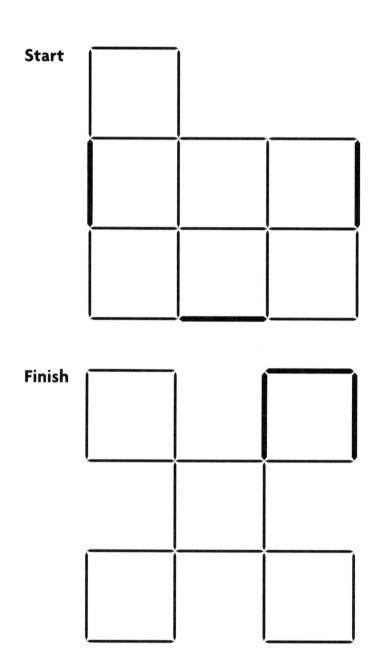

Lines, Shapes, and Numbers

How can you connect all the dots below and make the
bottom shape with **one** continuous stroke? You're not
allowed to trace over any lines!

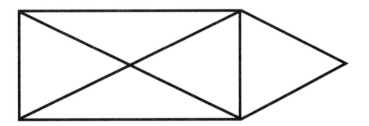

Start

Finish

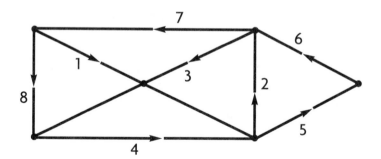

How can you connect all the dots below and make the bottom shape with **one** continuous stroke? You're not allowed to trace over any lines!

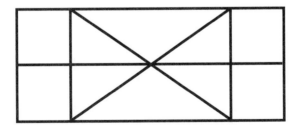

Start

Finish

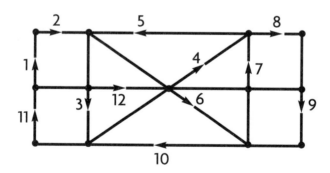

The equation below is incorrect, but it can be corrected by moving only **three** sticks on the left side of the equation. Which **three** sticks should you move?

Start

$$1351 - 900 = 1991$$

Finish

$$1191 + 800 = 1991$$

The equation below is incorrect, but it can be corrected by moving only **one** stick. Which stick should be moved?

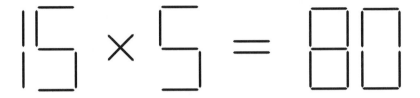

Start

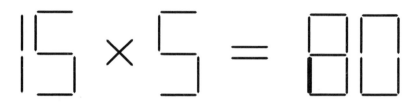

$15 \times 5 = 80$

Finish

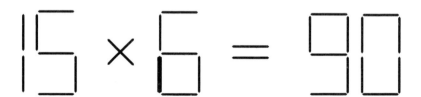

$15 \times 6 = 90$

Below are **two** shapes. **One** has already been divided into **two** halves. How can you divide the other into **two** pieces so that when the **four** pieces are put together you will form a square?

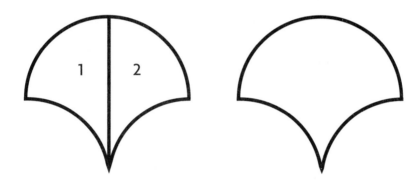

Start

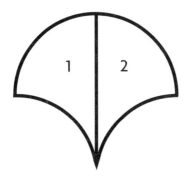

Step 1

Finish

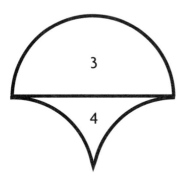

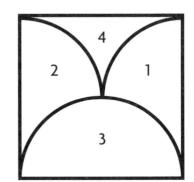

The pattern below is made up of **three** equal-size squares. There is a dot in the center of **one** square. Please draw a line over the dot so that the area on either side of the line will be equal.

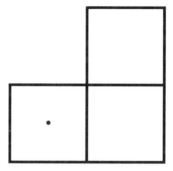

Start

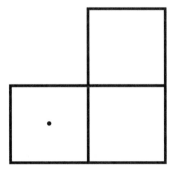

Finish

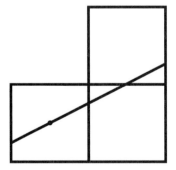

Please add the math symbols: +, −, ×, ( ), and = among the numbers **1** through **9** so that when you calculate the equation it will equal **100**.

1   2   3   4   5   6   7   8   9 = 100

Start

$$1 \quad 2 \quad 3 \quad 4 \quad 5 \quad 6 \quad 7 \quad 8 \quad 9 = 100$$

Finish

$$(1 + 2 + 3 + 4 + 5) \times 6 - 7 + 8 + 9 = 100$$

Please use **eight 8s** to form **five** numbers, then add
the **five** numbers together. The sum of the **five**
numbers should be **1,000.**

8   8   8   8   8   8   8   8

Start

8   8   8   8   8   8   8   8

Finish

888 + 88 + 8 + 8 + 8 = 1,000

When you add **one** line to **one** triangle, it turns into **three** triangles. When you add **two** lines, **six** triangles emerge. How many triangles will you have when you add **three** lines to the triangle?

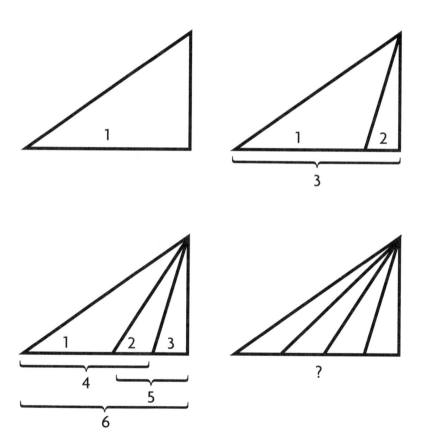

Start

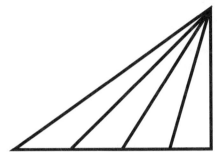

Finish

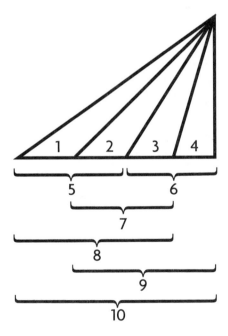

How many triangles are there in the pattern below?

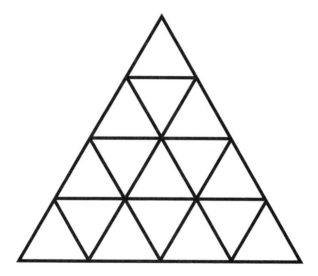

Start

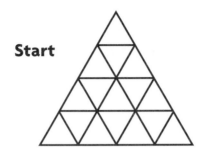

Finish There is a total of 27 triangles.

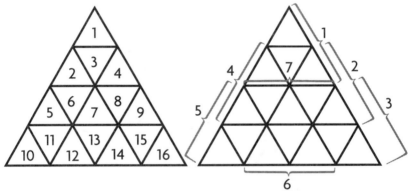

16 small ones

7, each made of 4 small ones

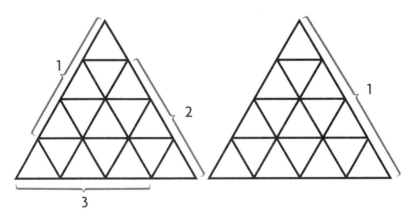

3, each made of 9 small ones

1, made of all 16 small ones

The number formed by these **three** blocks is **136.** This number cannot be divided by **7.** Please rearrange these **three** blocks so that the new number can be divided by **7.**

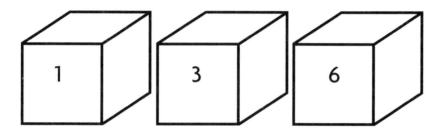

Start

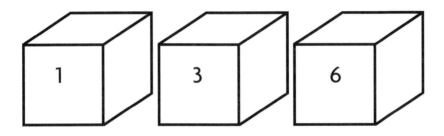

Finish

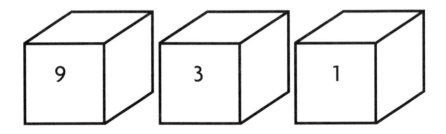

Each of the **six** sides of the following blocks is painted with a color. With these **three** sides shown, can you figure out the color of the opposite sides that are not shown?

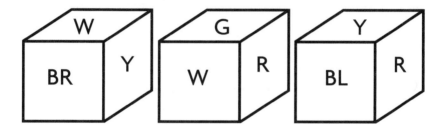

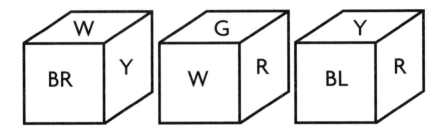

White is opposite blue;
red is opposite brown;
yellow is opposite green.

Find the pattern to the numbers in the circle below, then fill in the correct number in the empty space.

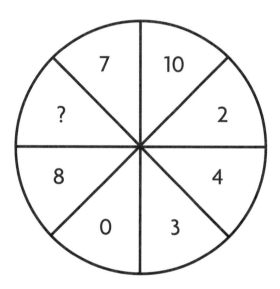

Start

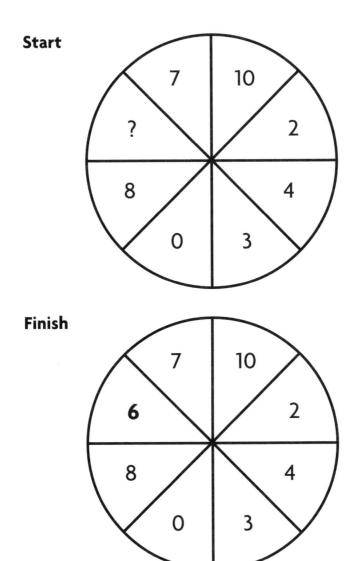

Finish

The correct number is **6.** (The sum of the numbers on opposite sides of the pie is **10.**)

Find the pattern to the numbers in the rectangle below, then fill in the correct number in the empty space.

9	8	5
81	64	25
63	48	?
Column 1	**Column 2**	**Column 3**

Start

Column 1	Column 2	Column 3
9	8	5
81	64	25
63	48	?

Finish

Column 1	Column 2	Column 3
9	8	5
81	64	25
63	48	**15**

The correct number is **15.** (The second number of each column minus double the first number equals the third number.)

Please fill in the numbers **1, 2, 3,** and **4** in the blank spaces below so that this math problem will make sense.

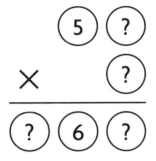

Start

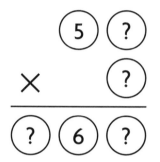

Finish

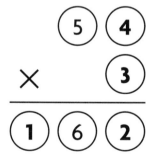

The **two** columns below are made up of circles with numbers in them. By switching **two** circles and adding a little cleverness, the sum of the **two** columns will become equal. How do you do this?

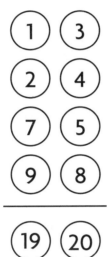

Start

Finish

Switch circles 8 and 9, and then flip the 9 to 6.

Take **ten** sticks and put them side by side. Pick up **one** stick and jump over **two** others to form a pair with a third stick. Make **five** separate jumps over two sticks to end up with five paired sticks. A pair of sticks counts as two as you jump over them. Hint: The first jump involves stick #4.

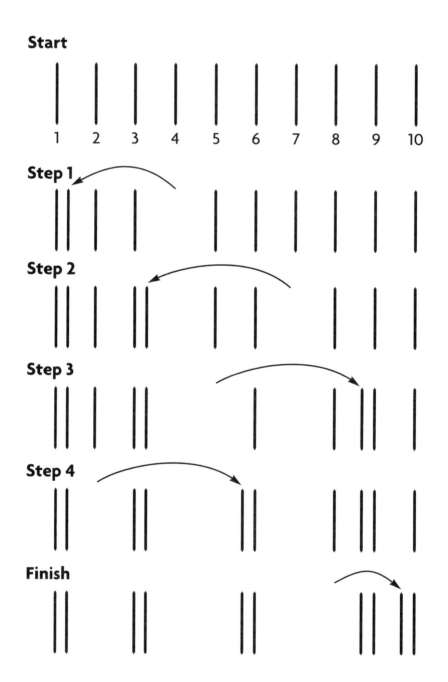

The pattern below consists of **one** big triangle and **three** small triangles. How do you fill in numbers **1** through **9** around the big triangle so that the sum of the numbers in the corners of each triangle equals **15**?

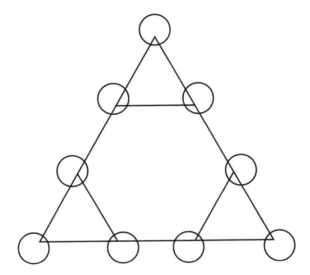

Start

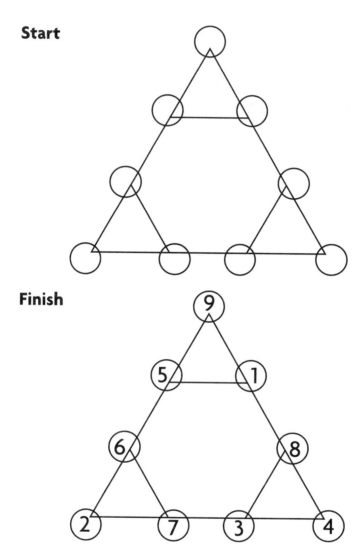

Finish

There is more than one arrangement of numbers that solves the puzzle, although the three corners of the big triangle must be 9, 2, and 4.

How can you fill in the **nine** small squares with numbers **1** through **9** so that the sum of all **three** numbers—horizontally, vertically, and diagonally— is the same?

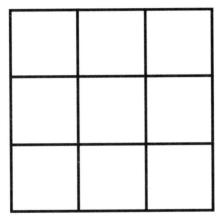

Start

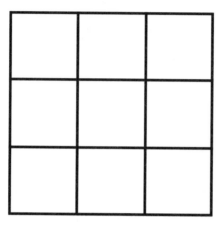

Finish

4	9	2
3	5	7
8	1	6

There is more than one arrangement of numbers that solves this problem.

Discover the pattern of how the numbers are increasing, then fill in the blank space.

Start

3 5 9 $?$ 23 33 45

Finish

3 5 9 $\mathbf{15}$ 23 33 45

$3 + 1 (2) = 5$; $5 + 2 (2) = 9$; $9 + 3 (2) = 15$; $15 + 4 (2) = 23$; and so on.

Connect these **five** chains together to form a big chain ring. Only **four** rings can be opened. How can you do this?

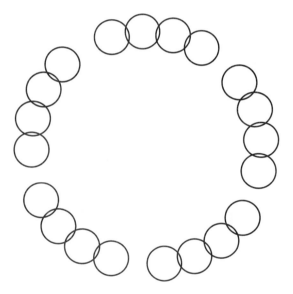

Start

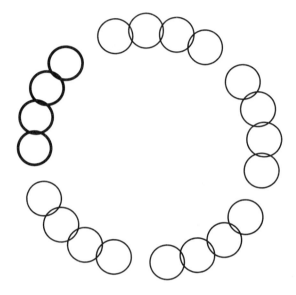

Finish

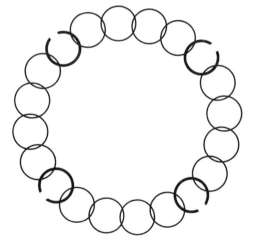

Open one chain of rings to connect the other **four** chains.

Remove a small triangle from both the white and the black portions of the pattern below. Then place the white triangle on the black side, and the black triangle on the white side, so that the pattern will turn into **two** fishes. Where do you cut then place the triangles?

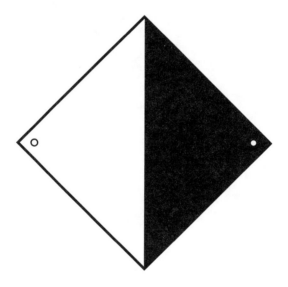

Start

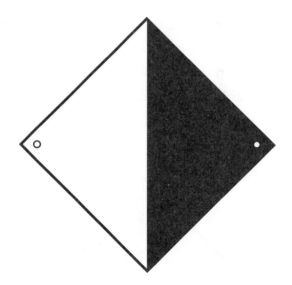

Finish

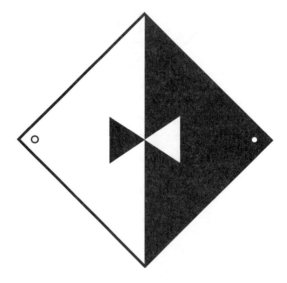

How do you separate the big H below into **five** pieces with two lines and then use those pieces to form a square?

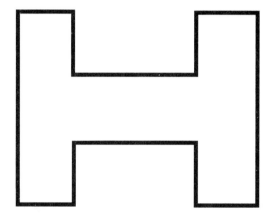

Start

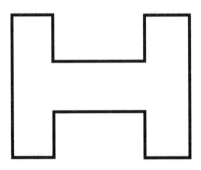

Step 1

Finish

You can separate the pattern below into **three** pieces and then use those pieces to form a **five**-pointed star. How can you do this?

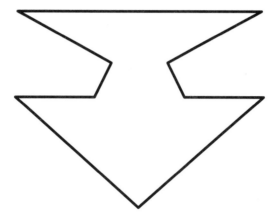

Start

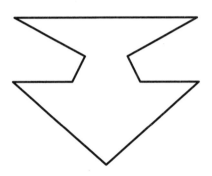

Step 1   **Finish**

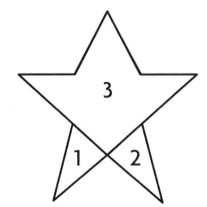

How do you separate the **two** squares into **four** pieces and then use those pieces to form **one** square?

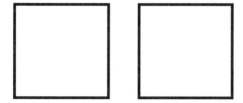

Start

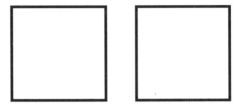

Step 1

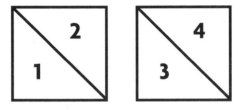

Finish

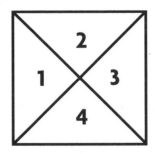